MAIDS, MADONNAS, & WITCHES

MAIDS,

&

Women in Sculpture

PHOTOGRAPHS BY ANDREAS FEININGER

MADONNAS, WITCHES

from Prehistoric Times to Picasso

INTRODUCTION BY **HENRY MILLER**

TEXT BY **J. BON**

Harry N. Abrams, Inc., Publishers, New York

Translated from the German by Joan Bradley
Library of Congress Catalog Card Number: 61-13859
All rights reserved. No part of the contents of this book
may be reproduced without the written permission
of Harry N. Abrams, Inc., New York
This book is published in association with
M. DuMont Schauberg, Cologne
Printed and bound in West Germany

Contents

Contents

Behold, thou art fair, my love; behold, thou art fair; thou
hast doves' eyes within thy locks; thy hair is as a flock of goats,
that appear from mount Gilead.

Thy teeth are like a flock of sheep that are
even shorn, which came up from the washing; whereof every
one bear twins, and none is barren among them.

Thy lips are like a thread of scarlet, and thy
speech is comely: thy temples are like a piece of pomegranate
within thy locks.

Thy neck is like the tower of David builded for an armoury, whereon
there hang a thousand bucklers, all shields of mighty men.

Thy two breasts are like two young roes that are twins, which
feed among the lilies.

Until the day break, and the shadows flee away, I will get me to
the mountain of myrrh, and to the hill of frankincense.

Song of Solomon, 4: 1–6

WOMAN THROUGHOUT THE AGES
by Henry Miller

ONE thing is certain—she has never been 'the weaker sex.' It is only in the last few thousand years—a mere nothing!—that man has seemed to dominate. I say 'seemed', for I find no evidence of real superiority or real domination on the part of man. He may make her over, in accordance with his ever changing ideals, but he never succeeds in truly subjugating her. As for woman, since the age of chivalry her effort to fashion man into her ideal image of man has been thoroughly frustrated. Certainly these athletes of today, these men of affairs, these leaders, poets, would be saints, these Neros and Alexanders can hardly represent a woman's ideal. Only the cinema stars possess a certain lure, a certain desired or imagined quality. Rudolph Valentino was definitely an ideal figure, but since then who can we name to rival him?

As for standards of beauty, though we find beauty in almost every race, it seems to me that the Polynesian and the Asiatic races show evidences of unchanging beauty. It is a racial beauty. In the case of the Polynesians and the Eurasians the admixture of other bloods only serves to enhance the ingrained beauty of the race. In Japan we see woman deliberately altering her physical features, and losing nothing of her ancient charm thereby, in order to enlarge her appeal.

As for what is called true femininity, undoubtedly the Oriental woman heads the list. As an example of womanhood the Japanese woman is extolled the world over. (The late Count Keyserling, who was no slouch in such matters, paid her the highest tribute.) And what of the Chinese, the Javanese, the Balinese women . . . has any one ever accused them of vulgarity, cheapness, masculine aggressiveness? The stupendous Chinese encyclopaedia, of which copies existed up until the Boxer rebellion, contained biographies, it is said, of over 40,000 famous Chinese women—famous in every walk of life. What can the Western world offer to match such a roll call?

Nothing could be more fallacious than to suppose that women are incapable, irresponsible, weak, fickle, and so on. In the Middle Ages, particularly during the Crusades when the important male figures were absent for long periods, it was the women who took over, who governed, who kept the arts alive—and hope and courage. France was particularly outstanding in this respect. In Africa the Tuareg woman is still a powerful, dominant figure. Even in India, where one imagines woman to play a negligible role, her power and influence are, to say the least, considerable. And what of those eccentric British queens whose names are now legendary? True, they do not give the impression of having the cultural stature of famous Chinese and Japanese empresses, but they ruled with a firm hand and more wisely than most kings. We are all familiar with the Amazons of old. Today a new type of Amazon has emerged. Today woman is taking her place beside man not only in field and factory but as a warrior. What a start we had when the Russians mustered their women to battle! Even now an involuntary shudder grips some of us when we see the Israeli woman, fully equipped, head high, marching in step beside her brother in arms. Why? Certainly not because she is weak or unfit. Perhaps because we know for certain now that the giver of life is also condemned to be the taker of life. Killing will no longer be the exclusive function of men. Yet women have always murdered as daringly, efficiently and monstrously as men, have they not? We have only to read, or reread, our history books, survey the lives of our queens and our women of noble blood. Long before the bloody days of the House of Atreus women were at it.

Which brings me to the crucial point. A woman is not a woman, nor a man a man, unless the male and female elements in each are well balanced. The women we so greatly admire are never simply big, beautiful cats; they have always a goodly element of masculinity in them. The same is true for men. The soft, flexible, poetic side—the dark side, as the Germans would say—must be there if the man is to hold and impress the woman. (Once again I think of Valentino, and as female counterpart Greta Garbo.)

We do not know, of course, what women were like, or men either, in the days prior to the emergence of *homo sapiens*. We are inclined to believe that they had a more integrated being than their successors. (From the very start *homo sapiens* gives the impression of being a schizoid.) Curious, is it not, that in the celebrated rock drawings of Spain and France there are no representations of men and women, only animals? We imagine that woman has remained essentially the same throughout the ages. (We should not overlook the fact that it is *men* who have delineated her nature, her attributes.)

Somewhere in his writings Walt Whitman has hinted at the great change which will come over the world—Rimbaud, too, for that matter—when women achieve real emancipation. He was not thinking of political or economic freedom, of that I am certain. He was thinking much like Lincoln, who once said: 'As I would not wish to be a slave, so I would not wish to be a master.'

If God created man in his own image man has certainly done his best to destroy the model. Among animals we have touching examples of conjugal love. As for men and women, all we know is ceaseless warfare, each trying to get the better of the other, with the result that they are chained to one another, as much the slave as the master of one another. Tradition, with its stupid codes and conventions, holds them as in a vise. Neither man nor woman has yet found the way to freedom. Freedom can only be found together, not separately, just as 'poetry must be made by all' (Lautréamont). The clue to eventual emancipation resides in our understanding, slowly developing, of male-female. Reverence for woman must not be based on some idolatrous attitude toward womanhood or motherhood but on the recognition that the female element is an inherent and essential part of man's being, that the two elements of our psyche are indivisible. In short, man, and by man I mean man-and-woman, must become aware of the full, the true, the significant nature of his being. Here I must remark in passing how often I have been impressed by the total beauty which is so often reflected in the countenances of Hindu men. Here, physically at least, we have intimations of the nature and aspect of the complete man, the man who realizes and gives expression to his dual nature. Seldom in the West do we observe this kind of beauty, unless it be among homosexuals, but the homosexual, though often fair to behold, is always in danger of being a caricature. In the animal world, as we know, it is the male which usually possesses the superior beauty. Now and again this same phenomenon is observable in the human world, witness the Berber or the Cretan man.

We speak of masculine wit, masculine courage, masculine ability, and of feminine charm, feminine treachery, feminine seductiveness, and so on. When will we learn to speak of *human* virtues or vices, acknowledging that they stem from male and female impartially?

And if we do become more human, which is to say more god-like, will not our standards of beauty, courage and so on change? We are living in an era characterized by swift, radical, irreversible changes. Why should *we* not change too? If once we began to look upon one another as brothers and sisters instead of members of races, nations, religions, political parties, would we not assume a different view of things, a different stance, a different physical aspect? We are what we think, and if we are obviously monstrous and abortive, there must be something amiss with our thinking. Perhaps we are laying the ground for our own dissolution, paving the way for the rise of a new, healthier, more integrated type of being. Perhaps the man of tomorrow will look in amazement at the specimens of beauty which we have so jealously preserved in the various media of art and literature; perhaps he will hold in derision the figures of our saints and heroes, our sages and wizards. Why not? Some of us are already able to do so. Man has long mocked the incredible pantheon of gods and goddesses he birthed. What is to prevent him from one day holding the mirror up to himself? No matter what the change, however, beauty will persist, and wit and courage, and hope and faith.

THE **F**ACE. On the next few pages we shall encounter the face of Woman, always different, yet eternally feminine, woman as goddess and as human being, as symbol and as portrait. As symbol or idol of sublime earnestness, it represents everything human, the embodiment of religious feeling and early conceptions of faith.

It is not the woman of any specific era, not a unique creation, that faces us in the small ivory head of the Early Stone Age or in the abstract faces of the Cycladic culture; we must regard them rather as symbolic representations, developed and solidified in the material over thousands of years—until contemporary times in the faces of the Senufo and Bambara sculptures of Africa.

Only in the latter stages of the great cultures did the face become a portrait, a reflection of an individual personality.

The path to full knowledge and understanding of past or foreign civilisations is often difficult to follow, since we are looking for two different things: the meaning and content of former religious concepts, presented to us figuratively in these faces, as well as the artistic form of their representation, their visual beauty. Every face poses the question: why was it conceived and portrayed in this particular way? We wish to read these faces, to divine the thoughts behind them, to understand their times and, above all, to find out what it was that inspired the artist who formed the face in stone, wood, bronze or clay.

It is important to remember that the stronger the spiritual reality of the abstraction, the further removed it is from the individual personality. While exact portraiture denotes man in isolation, abstraction presents the connection between the visible and, more important, invisible powers of being. It is not woman the object of our love who is portrayed, but a being superior to every conception of its own age, the mother of mankind, the female as fundamental vision and as creator, as the symbol of fertility.

From the dim and distant past the small Stone Age face of an ivory figure gazes at us (plate 5). This face has no mouth, the eyes are deeply sunken under the forehead; they seem to watch us, yet we cannot return the look. It is not only the age of this small head that awes us; the timeless expression casts a stronger spell. Brought to light again after thousands of years, this face confronts us with numerous riddles, for it exudes a profound feeling of life. Already in these earliest times an important feature of the female face took shape: the sorrow of the world arising from the knowledge of the destiny of all creation. It is woman as prophetess.

Thousands of years later, the severe yet spell-binding Cycladic head was shaped (plate 1). Just a flat disc, with a slight allusion to a nose, it represents a high degree of abstraction, completely removed from the reality of the natural model. It would be quite wrong to hold up this head as an example of 'primitive' art. It expresses a power of intensification and spiritualisation which has only been regained in this form of composition about 5,000 years later in the great creations of our own century. It seems that life on the small islands of ancient times, distant and cut off from the rest of the world as they were, encouraged contemplation and meditation.

But what a different spirit animates the face of Nefertiti (plate 3), a portrait statue of the 18th dynasty of Ancient Egypt (with which the New Kingdom began). This statue also remains strictly true to the traditions of the age, yet comes very near to realistic portraiture. The woman is no longer a symbol, but a Queen, wife of the King, self-assured, conscious of her position and of the power and tradition of a divine kingship thousands of years old, rooted in a belief which her husband, Akhenaten, was the first to turn away from.

We encounter yet another world, the Hellenic, in the head of the terra-cotta figure from the second century B.C. (plate 4). With the Greeks the divine becomes human, therefore human characteristics are accorded the dignity and awe of the divine. They formed their gods like the most beautiful and well-proportioned human beings, who possess no supermundane qualities, but instead enjoy eternal youth. The Greek artist was not interested in reproducing the individual, with all his or her shortcomings. He preferred his creations in their full beauty; therefore, since he idealised them, in his mind they became abstract.

One must browse slowly through these pictures, continually referring back. Like the pre-Columbian heads from Mexico (plates 13, 15), many of the African ones (plates 9, 12, 14), show little likeness to nature; indeed, we may search in vain for any typically feminine characteristics. These are often totally lacking; the face is, at best, simply human.

Many of the works, such as the sculptures of the Baule tribe in Africa (plate 16), express tenderness and feminity. In others, as for instance the flat faces of the Bakota tribe's figures, the facial features are so abstract that the sexes are indistinguishable (plates 17, 18). Even the natives cannot help us to understand them. Dumb and unapproachable, these faces reign over the tribe's most sacred shrines; they guard the skulls and bones of its revered ancestors and protect them from the prying eyes of strangers. The mother of mankind watches over the forefathers.

The picture of woman the sufferer finds its most moving and authentic representation during the Middle Ages in the form of the sorrowing Mother of God (plate 19). Her face reflects every sorrow women have borne and bear to this day. She is resigned to the fate imposed upon her. In the pain she suffers at the death of her Son we feel the pain of all women and mothers; their silent indictment of a world of suffering.

Every perception and feeling, every belief and doubt—indeed, every unanswered question—is reflected in the faces of these women. They have a permanence, a continuous affinity one with the other through the most distant times and cultures. If we are prepared to listen, they speak to us. And when they speak, they disclose more of man's thoughts during his long history, more of his struggles to become attuned to the powers of good and evil, than we would learn from any other source.

I THE FACE

14

15

THE **E**TERNAL POSE. Is this really a pose in the accepted sense of the word: an attitude devised for a certain effect? In fact, it is not, for in these pictures we see a symbolic form of expression as old as time itself: the symbol of fertility.

Ever since men became settlers and started to live from the fruits of the land they tilled, they have turned their thoughts to the forces which, in their opinion, influenced the mystery of birth and death in human life and in Nature. That is why they endowed woman, whom they knew in person as mother and nourisher, with this supernatural and divine power. From this sprang the cult of the Great Mother, the Earth Goddess, which continued for thousands of years. The motif of the mother of mankind, offering her breasts to the world with both hands, portrays a deep, fundamental belief.

One of the oldest extant examples is the idol of fertility from Ur (plate 22), part of the Sumerian culture on which our Western civilisation is founded. From the Near East this religion of the 'magna mater' spread westwards and north=wards to Scandinavia and England.

The simple wood-carving from the Cameroons (plate 27) may date from almost five thousand years later, but the pose and the message remain the same: both of them symbolise fertility, the nourishment the mother carries for the helpless child, a most fundamental, yet at the same time a most wonderful function of woman.

From another part of the world, from the sphere of the Central American civilisations, comes the rather crudely fashioned Costa Rican figure (plate 32). The religion of these peoples, too, arose from the communion with the powers of Nature, from their fear of these powers and their attempts to keep them within bounds. Although in later times the male reigned supreme in the world of divinities, the events in Nature were first symbolised by the female, whom the people endowed with their own human traits. Clay figurines of this sort were not only placed in tombs, but were also set up for venera-tion in special niches in the huts and houses. This in due course led to the maize goddesses of the Aztecs, youthful, beautiful beings who cared for the safety of the food most important for life—maize.

What deep seriousness is expressed by the wooden sculpture from Easter Island (plate 35), despite its clumsy appearance! We sense that the carver's hand was moved by a strong religious feeling; he was not concerned with reproducing the

thy wrists
are holy
which are the keepers of the keys of thy blood
thy feet upon thy ankles are flowers
in vases of silver

in thy beauty is the dilemma of flutes

thy eyes are the betrayal
of bells comprehended through incense

E. E. Cummings

beauty of the feminine form. These figures were covered with pieces of bark. Only during rare festivals were they brought out of the huts and worshipped in ceremonies and dances. It is the ancestors who are realized in these rigid postures.

The Medici-type Venus (plate 36) shows the same outward pose as the figure from Easter Island, but the two sculptures are divided by continents and centuries. The Venus is no longer the awe-inspiring mother goddess, but the Greek interpretation of the perfect, beautiful female being, the goddess in eternal youth, in idealised human form. Inclining slightly with a coquettish gesture, she is aware of the charm of her body. Her attitude stems from the ancient symbolic tradition, but it has become nothing but a 'pose'. Her hands no longer describe the beliefs of a religious cult; nor do they hide anything, but rather consciously indicate her own beauty—and incidentally make us aware that some of the charm of the early figures has been lost.

II THE ETERNAL POSE

29

MOTHERHOOD

OTHERHOOD. Motherhood inspires the purest and most durable of human thoughts and emotions. Most of the ideals man has created during his historical development have sooner or later become questionable and meaningless. One alone has endured from the beginning of creation to the present day: the ideal of motherhood which combines love and care, self-sacrifice and self-denial, happiness and fulfilment. From it man draws the strength to meet all life's challenges. Where this ideal was neglected, there also society and its culture crumbled.

The forms used to express motherhood result from combining two separate ideas: that of Mother Earth, nourishing Man, and that of the human mother, who conceives, carries, gives birth to, cares for and protects the child.

In the Western world the essence of motherhood was expressed in its purest and most noble form in the Madonna of medieval art. The pose of the Flemish Mary in the Early Gothic style (plate 55) still has something of the stiff, superhuman majesty of Early Christian art, with its detachment from life and preoccupation with the spirit, yet her face displays human emotion and we find her expression touching.

The fourteenth-century ivory statue exudes a wonderful charm amd warmth; full of trust and intimacy, the child reaches lovingly for his mother's face (plate 38).

More down-to-earth and homely is the Burgundian Madonna who, with a motherly gesture, offers her breast to the tired Child (plate 56).

The Swedish wood-carving of the late Middle Ages shows the Queen of Heaven, more stern and distant, but still vulnerable in her innermost being (plate 54).

The theme of mother and child is much older than the familiar Christian representation. Thousands of years earlier it was the goddess Isis, embodiment of all fertility, with the boy Horus on her knee, who was the mother-figure (plate 51).

In Babylon and India, too, divine women, mothers of divinities, are reproduced in the same way but conforming to the style of their civilisation. Although elevated to the divine, they express an aspect of humanity. In a sense the divine becomes visible in this earthly form. In this picture of eternal motherhood, Heaven and Earth are joined (plates 39, 40).

Ich sehe dich in tausend Bildern,
Maria, lieblich ausgedrückt,
Doch keins von allen kann dich schildern,
Wie meine Seele dich erblickt.

Ich weiss nur, dass der Welt Getümmel
Seitdem mir wie ein Traum verweht
Und ein unnennbar süsser Himmel
Mir ewig im Gemüte steht.

Novalis

Of thee a thousand portraits rare
In adoration men have wrought,
Yet not, O Mary, the most fair
Can match the image in my heart.

And I give thanks that when this leaven
The world's disquiet like a dream
Dissolved, an unimagined heaven
Encompassed me with azure flame.

Translation by Eric Peters

Goddess and venerated ancestress alike, the maternal statue from the civilisations of coastal India watches us with strangely penetrating eyes (plate 39). We encounter her again in Melanesia, where, though awkwardly carved and highly stylized in the details, she radiates a similar fervour while protecting her small child (plate 46).

One of the most motherly women in the world—a fact always particularly stressed by Europeans—is the African, the Negress. There are not many countries where the child is so lovingly cared for, or so rarely punished with harsh words, let alone a blow. The theme of motherhood extends in a variety of forms throughout the whole of Africa, here true to nature, there more abstract; sometimes the child is carried in the mother's arms or, according to tribal custom, on her back or her hips; more often she is nursing it.

Beside these truly animated African figures the pre-Columbian forms from Mexico appear more rigid and for-bidding—one is tempted to say, more ritual. But even here, when the goddess or divine mother and her son are portrayed in the purest form, the deep human feeling in this theme appeals to us with great immediacy and allows us to forget differences in time and place.

III MOTHERHOOD

P

ROVOCATION AND VANITY. Another side of the female character, just as real as the maternal one, is that which takes pleasure in adornment, in dress and make-up. This is not always primarily for her own enjoyment but also for that of the male, and therefore a necessity for the woman, a kind of weapon in the conquest of the opposite sex and in defence against her own. Moreover, when one looks back over the amount of jewellery fashioned and worn by human beings during the course of time, one finds that woman still has much to do to overtake man. To give but one example: the wealth found in Peruvian tombs belonged, with few exceptions, to men who by custom were adorned with numerous chains of gold and gems. Only during the last few centuries has Western woman surpassed man with the splendour of her jewels.

The same applies to make-up and dress. Thus it is, for instance, often difficult—especially in African work—to discern from a figure's hair style and ornament alone whether it represents a woman. Both sexes love to take elaborate care of their hair. Every female statue shown here had a male counterpart. The desire for adornment is present in every human being, and the same can be said for vanity.

Various examples of dress, ornaments and hair-styles should give us an insight into the different ways in which the 'eternal Eve' was regarded. Periods of advanced urban civilisation are, naturally, particularly productive, and the sculpture of the late Middle Ages provide us with a life-like impression of how the lady of society looked in those days. The statue of a saint of 1520 shows dress and jewellery in the minutest detail (plate 58). If we did not know that this came from an altar, and if the figure did not carry the traditional attributes of a saint, we might take it for the portrait of a young lady from a wealthy merchant's family. Nor would we be entirely wrong; for despite his sacred commission the medieval artist had an eye for the fashions and beauty of his time. A whole world divides this saint from the profoundly and strictly religious works of the early Middle Ages.

Through the ages women have devoted loving care and attention to their hair, often assisting Nature with sumptuous wigs, as even the Egyptian statue of the 18th dynasty shows (plate 59). Today's Negress spends much time and trouble on the same things; she needs the help of a particularly clever friend, in order to achieve her artistic, often fantastic, hair-style (plates 60—62). She, too, has recourse to small artificial means of appearing fashionable and elegant. One

A garden enclosed is my sister, my spouse;
a spring shut up, a fountain sealed.

Thy plants are an orchard of pomegranates, with pleasant
fruits; camphire, with spikenard.

Spikenard and saffron; calamus and cinnamon, with all trees of
frankincense; myrrh and aloes, with all the chief spices;

A fountain of gardens, a well of living waters, and streams
from Lebanon.

Song of Solomon, 4:12-15

must not think of primitive peoples as unconcerned about fashion; in the absence of frequent changes in clothing, changing fashion finds expression in imaginative coiffures. The examples from West Africa provide an eloquent testimony.

To satisfy the need for ornamentation and the aesthetic sense of many African tribes, embellishment of the body is essential. They daub themselves for festivals—mainly in accordance with ritual requirements—and they also submit to painful tattooing. It is not surprising, therefore, that in sculpture these highly ornamented bodies are most carefully reproduced by the carver. Often these patterns help to identify the figure as from a certain tribe. But even here one finds quirks of fashion which depart from the decorations laid down by tribal custom.

Some of the most richly-ornamented statues are those of the Bena Lulua, whose faces, necks and bodies contain hardly a single unadorned spot. One of the ideals of beauty among the African Negro tribes is the prominent navel, as is clearly demonstrated by the Senufo statue (plate 71).

Down the ages not only women, but men also, have been ready suffer agonies for the sake of fashion, in order to be 'beautiful'. Nobody ever seemed to ask whether it was comfortable to burden the ears with numerous rings or to fasten a heavy ring to the nose, as fashion demanded in ancient Mexico. And how much more uncomfortable it must have been to splay the lips to the size of plates by wearing broad wooden plugs, in the manner shown by the Makonde mask (plate 69). It is worth noting that other tribes who practise this same custom of lip plugs explain that the men used this means of deforming their women and girls to protect them from slave traders. Yet, long after the departure of slave hunters from Africa, the women of these tribes clung to their uncomfortable 'adornment'. In Africa today, there are only a very few old women left to remind us of this deformity, which to our eyes is so hideous. The same may happen in the case of tattooing, as the younger generation no longer willingly submits to the long-drawn-out and painful process when the allure of gay European materials is so much greater.

As well as tattooing, painting of the body plays an important part. Where this is fixed by ritual, the women of the primitive peoples are overshadowed by the men; once the initiation ceremonies are over, their later life offers few opportunities for painting themselves. To this rule the wood-carving from New Guinea provides an exception (plate 66).

IV PROVOCATION AND VANITY

59

69

71

ABSTRACT FORMS AND DISTORTIONS.

The use of these terms in a chapter heading does not imply an aesthetic evaluation, but a process instigated by the artist, the creator, who was usually inspired by a strong religious feeling. For us, both abstract treatment and distortions signify a conscious handling of a work of art.

Almost all the figures shown in this chapter can only be understood if we are prepared to put aside our classically schooled sense of form and endeavour to gauge each work by its own inner conformity with the rules. Nor must we be satisfied with the allure of the 'exotic', which may gloss over what is important and prevent us from forming our own point of view.

Over-emphasis of a particular part of the body is a fundamental characteristic of the Stone Age figurine, but it only applies to the representations of the female. These small, broad-hipped figures with heavy breasts and mere suggestions of faces were found almost all over Europe; the countenances of these fertility idols seem to be sunk in primordial mists; they do not yet represent an individual, but have the neutral expression of the Great Mother, who, impersonal and omnipotent, acts as the giver of life.

It is somewhat misleading that these figures have been christened 'Venuses', a name which generally suggests to our minds quite different concepts. These are without doubt sacred figures, imbued with magical powers, whose forms have nothing to do with the ideals of beauty of the Stone Age hunters, as has been maintained in certain quarters. This concept was never important in the earliest cultures. This becomes even clearer if one looks at contemporary cave paintings as a comparison. The vivid naturalism of such drawings reveals the acute powers of observation possessed by those men, and consigns the figures of women to a magico-religious sphere, in which fidelity to nature was never intended. Certainly the cave paintings are also founded on religious ideas, but on concepts of a different kind from those which gave these female forms an exaggeratedly maternal look, even a semblance of pregnancy, the symbol of the continuity of life and of the prosperity of the community. The representation of a pregnant woman repels some of us, as if it violated a taboo. For centuries our eye, although subject to fashion changes, has been accustomed to the sight of a well-proportioned feminine figure. During the nineteenth century especially, pregnancy was something to be completed as far as possible 'in secret'. People preferred to ignore the ungainly body, and felt that the event should remain within the circle of the family. Even today, few people dwell on the thought that the birth of a human being is full of the deepest symbolism, in which human life and permanence are reflected.

This symbolic background cannot be sufficiently stressed, for it alone allows us a full understanding of the many 'distorted' figures in most of the early cultures of both the Old and the New Worlds.

They are almost always small figures made of clay—during the late Palaeolithic Age sometimes of soft limestone or mammoth tooth—for clay offered the first easily manipulated material. Apart from clay fragments, such small female figures are all that remains of many early cultures, and are therefore often all that we have to grant us an insight into their religious beliefs.

Since trading over long distances began quite early, it is not surprising that finds in the Near East and in India should show remarkable similarity.

On the other hand, the figures from the Cyclades (plates 82, 83) are readily distinguished from all others; their composition is more abstract, more spiritualized, confined to a mere suggestion of a face, from which the nose protrudes in relief, and to a vaguely-defined body.

A characteristic feature of many figures from the New World is the flat receding brow, an appearance artificially achieved by binding the child's skull and required by ritual or tradition.

Heads and faces are shown in detail, often covered with ornaments, the arms arranged in a variety of positions; most of these sculptures have one thing in common—an over-emphasis of the breasts and hips.

The pre-dynastic Egyptian dancers are an exception (plates 80, 81). These figures are elongated, and the position of the arms is always exactly the same; only their breasts are indicated in a natural way, while their hands turn inwards to resemble wings, and their faces, scarcely formed, are more reminiscent of a bird than of a human being.

Their meaning is a matter for conjecture, as is that of the Swedish Bronze Age figures (plate 108), about two thousand years later. We know of no tradition that would help to explain it.

In stark contrast to the swollen bodies of the early clay figures are the examples from the Ashanti tribe (plate 109) and

East Africa (plate 103). A huge facial disc dominates the Ashanti figures; the body becomes a mere pole, often even without breasts. The body also serves as a handle. These figures, however, are definitely idols of fertility and are carried on the backs of women wishing to be blessed with children. Generally, the Ashanti artist does not favour any abstract treatment; this constitutes an exception in the art of the African native. Their famous brass weights for weighing gold show lively and emphatically three-dimensional scenes. We see, then, how careful we must be in our interpretations. There is no typical goddess of fertility.

Even the uses to which such figures were put varied: as offerings, buried in the fields to entreat growth for the crops, or as fertility amulettes carried around or set up in the house. Or again, they were often burial gifts.

Their religious meaning, especially in later civilizations, tended to be relegated to the background; the charming Tanagra figures from Hellenistic times (plate 111) are a case in point.

There is no way of telling why many of these forms should show such peculiar distortions. But although—so strange do they seem to our eyes—we can offer them little understanding, the genius which shaped them still commands our awe.

V ABSTRACT FORMS AND DISTORTIONS

94

95 9

THE T ORSO. Since Rodin the idea that the word torso meant only an incomplete or partly preserved figure has been dispelled. Modern art recognises the torso as a consciously constructed shape, as a complete creation, confined to essentials.

It is therefore not easy to compare a modern torso, like that by Alberto Viani (plate 120), with fragments of antique statues (see plate 113). In the former, there has been voluntary renunciation by the sculptor: with transcendent perception he has reduced the female body to a few flowing lines, not copying Nature, but creating a new form. In the latter, we must re-create the lost parts in our imagination; since the passing of time has clearly affected these works, we are impelled to investigate the existing pieces more closely: we touch the folds of the clothing, we examine the delicate moulding of the surface, the curves of the body, or a bow on a dress or a tendril of hair on the second-century B.C. statue of Hygeia (plate 117). By doing so we discover how unimportant the face often is; the masterful reproduction of the body under a robe which reveals the figure rather than veiling it from our inquisitive eyes, as in the Hellenistic Hygeia, allows us to forget that only a fragment remains of what the artist had in mind.

It is more difficult to find an approach to the ancient Mexican figures (plate 115). Although their heads have been lost, their torsos have never the same impact as modern statues. The strongly moulded breasts and the massive thighs remind us that even here religious conceptions determined the shape. On the other hand, the Indian torso from a shrine in Sanchi (plate 118) exercises a direct appeal with its suggestion of a combined modesty and fervour.

VI   THE TORSO

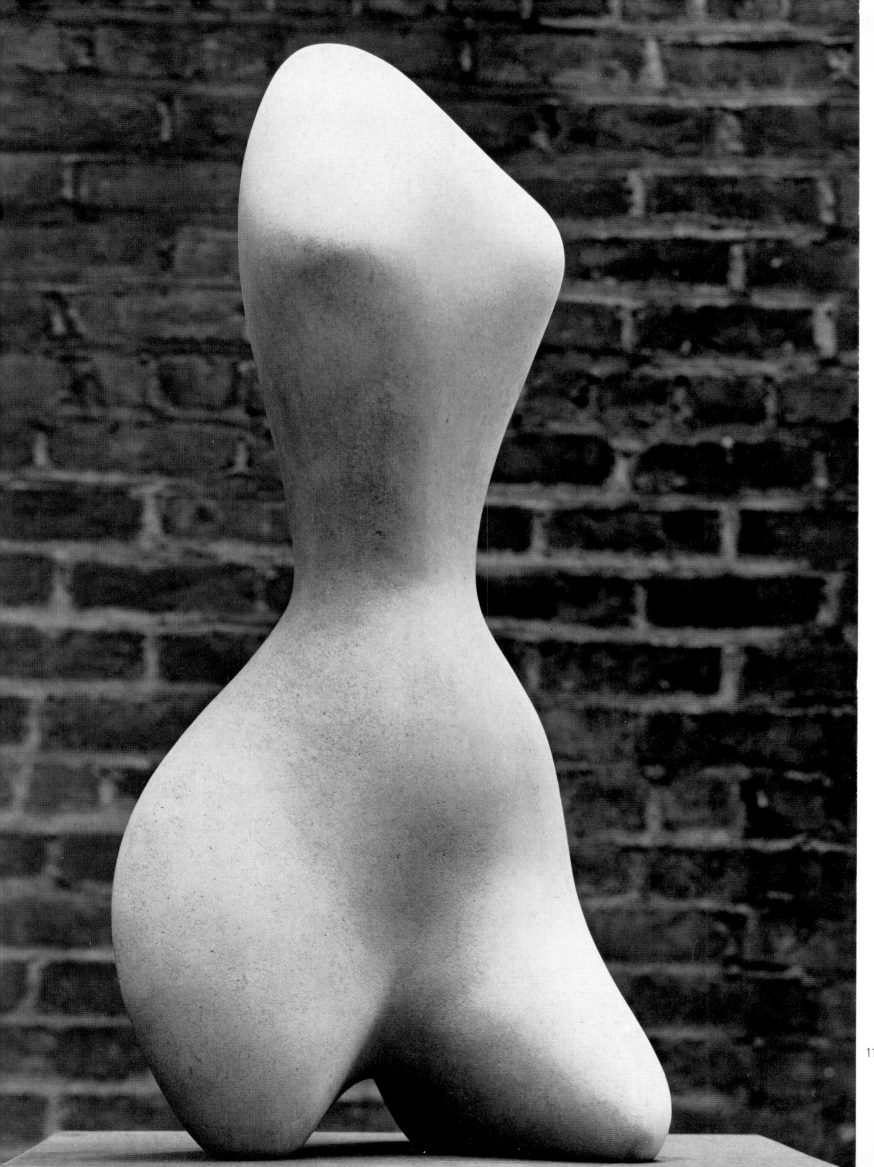

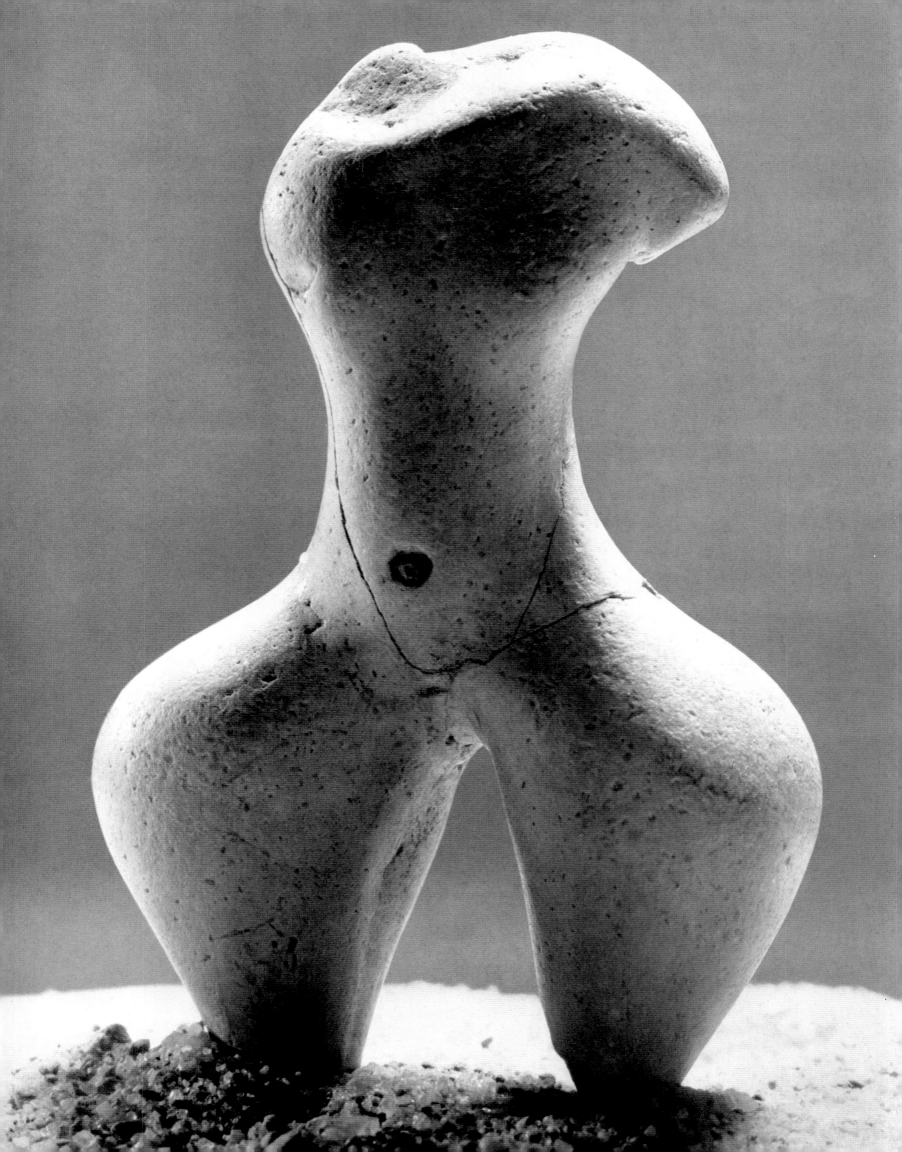

118

CLASSIC FORMS. In most primitive cultures, painting and sculpture never forsake the religious theme. In advanced civilisations alone, and then only after long development, does art free itself to disclose every facet of life. Only then can we speak of an ideal of beauty as such.

Is the ideal of feminine beauty the same in all ages and civilisations? The answer to this question greatly depends on whether the questioner's viewpoint is that of the artist or the man. Classical Greece provided the Western world with its model. Although subject to changes in fashion and also certain regional deviations, for the most part the soft, full curves of the classic female body, of a Venus de Milo, are admired and emulated. The ideal, the dream, throughout the rest of the world varies according to race and creed, changes in taste and foreign influences.

Beside the reassuringly touchable form of a Greek Aphrodite the Egyptian female statues, following the rules of their style, seem far less corporeal (plates 122, 123). But if, for example, one examines the stone torso of the 4th dynasty more attentively (plate 116), one comes to see the sublime interplay of the surfaces which make up the female form. The transition from the naked body to the robe, which only becomes clearly visible round the legs, is effortless. The latter clings to the hips like a second skin, revealing the delicate curves of the body. In contrast to the Greek figures, so full of life, the Egyptian ones seem more subtle, somewhat fragile despite their firmness. This may be due to the stylization, which captured the essential, the ideal pattern, while doubtless also rendering the picture these people had of the ideal woman. The Indian figure seems to us exotic. Voluptuous breasts, a slim waist and rounded hips characterize Indian sculpture (plate 128), traits which remind us of the small idols of early times. But their archetypal features have been banished by the refinement with which this body was made, the graceful pose of the hands—determined by ritual—the elegant hairstyle and the sumptuous ornaments.

Even in the ritual female figure an age's ideal of beauty was occasionally expressed. This is certainly true of the later, Hellenistic period of Etruscan art (plate 127). Although archaeologists may declare that the figures were created to serve a cult, their charm — and not only to the contemporary eye — lies in the homage they pay to the unspoilt beauty of woman, the beauty of her face as well as her body.

We encounter the image of an ideal, which portrays the female body in playful elegance, free from any religious impli-

Schreitest unter deinen Fraun
Und du lächelst oft beklommen:
Sind so bange Tage kommen.
Weiß verblüht der Mohn am Zaun.

Wie dein Leib so schön geschwellt
Golden reift der Wein am Hügel.
Ferne glänzt des Weihers Spiegel,
Und die Sense klirrt im Feld.

In den Büschen rollt der Tau,
Rot die Blätter niederfließen.
Seine liebe Frau zu grüßen,
Naht der Mohr dir braun und rauh.

Georg Trakl

There among your women pacing
All uneasily you smile:
Anxious days spent joys replacing.
Poppies bleach beneath the stile.

Round and mellow like your belly
Vines grow gold upon the hills.
Gleams the water in the valley,
Scythe-enmeshed the ripe corn spills.

Glisten diamond dewdrops fleeting,
Rust-red leaves spin from the bough;
His dear Lady bent on greeting
Blackamoor advances now.

Translation by Eric Peters

cations, in the statuettes of the lesser German masters during the sixteenth century (plate 130). The joy in creating these forms is, perhaps, even more obvious in the works of the French sculptors of that time, Goujon (plate 131) and Pilon (plate 121) having left us the most beautiful.

What of our own time? Is our ideal reproduced in the works of, say, Picasso? His creations and those of other notable modern artists cannot be drawn into a discussion on the ideal of beauty. The aim of the contemporary artist is to express meaning; he makes everything else subordinate to this.

VII CLASSIC FORMS

125

127

132

WOMAN IN MODERN SCULPTURE.

In the previous chapters we stated that only in a later phase of development did art free itself from religion. Now modern art also deviates from a natural pattern, for it is no longer modelled on Nature. Contemporary artists create their own world. They are fascinated by form and all its many potentialities; they are no longer interested in the outward aspects of life, but seek to express its purpose and meaning. So the human figure, for centuries the ultimate goal and the predominant theme of sculpture, is also included in this search—in this new task. Forms become more and more estranged from Nature, which is now no more than a source of inspiration and is changed by the artist to express his own ideas of form.

This development began at the end of the last century and led to the wholly abstract work of the contemporary sculptors. When his eyesight started to fail Degas (plate 134) carved numerous statues, many of which, unfortunately, have been destroyed. In clay and wax, he re-created his jockeys, dancers, and bathers—images which remained in his mind's eye. With great mastery he translated the forms he used in his paintings with their tense poses and cunning balance into three-dimensional terms.

Wilhelm Lehmbruck's 'Kneeling Woman' (1911) soon became famous (plate 133). This figure, with her more than life-sized, straight, almost too thin limbs, her thoughtful attitude, and her shape reduced to bare essentials, radiates a tranquil spirituality.

What a contrast it is to the voluptuousness of Maillol (plate 135), who was the most classic sculptor of his generation and who combined Greek severity with French charm.

Henri Laurens (plate 136) belonged to the Cubist school. In his works sculpture reverts to the cosmic elements; he fits the human shape to the rhythm of his material, thereby achieving pure movement.

Marino Marini is the most famous contemporary Italian sculptor. In the powerful moulding of his statues, which combine true naivety with independence, he revives the spirit of late Antiquity (plate 137).

Henri Matisse played just as important a part in the birth of modern sculpture as he did in the development of painting. His works illustrate the French school of Expressionism in sculpture (plate 138).

VIII WOMAN IN MODERN SCULPTURE

Notes on the Plates

I THE FACE

1 Marble head from the Cyclades

Second millennium B.C. Guennol Collection, New York. The Cyclades are a group of islands forming a circle around Delos, the Aegean birthplace of Apollo. The early Bronze Age civilisation of the Cyclades, beginning in the second half of the third millennium, produced many idols, mostly female, sculptured in the local marble. These statues, which were also produced in countries bordering on the Aegean, are sometimes as large as three-quarters life-size.

2 Portrait of a young Egyptian woman

Fourteenth century B.C. Museum of Fine Arts, Boston. Egypt became a world power under the kings of the 18th dynasty (1580—1330). The greatest ruler was Amenhotep III. This statue probably portrays the daughter of a high official at the Pharaoh's court.

3 Head of Nefertiti, Egypt

Probably one of the most famous heads of all time. The exceptionally fine features, the delicate neck, the elegantly shaped eyes and straight nose provide us even today, after thirty-four centuries, with the striking portrait of a noble, self-assured personality. Nefertiti was the wife of King Amenhotep IV (about 1375–1358), who called himself Akhenaten and strove for religious reform in favour of Aten, the sun-god.

4 Head of a Greek terra-cotta figure

Second century B.C. Museum of Fine Arts, Boston. During the second century, the so-called Hellenistic period of Greek art, the development of idyllic features coincided with the conquering of the territories of Diadochi.

5 Small Early Stone Age ivory head, Aurignacian, France

About 20,000 B.C. Saint-Germain-en-Laye. A gripping early representation of a woman in whose features we seem to recognise the eternal prophetess.

6 Portrait of Queen Hatshepsut, Egypt

Life-size granite statue. 18th dynasty, fourteenth century B.C. Metropolitan Museum of Art, New York. Hatshepsut played a part in the confusion which prevailed after the accession of Tuthmosis III to the throne. Palestine, Syria and Nubia were conquered by Egypt; Thebes became the capital of the world.

7 Head of St Anne, France

Sandstone figure of the Late Gothic school in Troyes. About 1510. Metropolitan Museum of Art, New York. An example of extreme humility and motherliness, St Anne, the wife of St Joachim and the mother of Mary, is the patron saint of mothers.

8 Marble head from the Cyclades

Third millennium B.C. Guennol Collection, New York. See note on plate 1.

9 Head of a wooden figure from the Senufo tribe, Africa
    American Museum of Natural History, New York.
The Senufo are a tribe of small cattle-breeders in ex-French Guinea and on the Ivory Coast. Their artistic sculptures and masks are famous.

10 Head of a Bambara wood-carving, Africa
    Carlebach Gallery, New York.
Bambara was originally a native kingdom in ex-French Sudan, covering both sides of the Upper Niger and with Sagu-Sikoro as its capital.

11 Head of a Basonge wood-carving, Africa
    Partly copper-mounted. Carlebach Gallery, New York.
The Basonge tribe belongs to the Bantu of the southern Congo.

12 Head of a Baluba wood-carving, Africa
    Nineteenth century. Peabody Museum, Cambridge, Mass.
The facial characteristics and the fine workmanship suggest that this figure originates from this tribe's most important centre of carving, Buli in the southern Congo region.

13 Head of a clay figure from Western Mexico (Nayarit)
    With ornamented nose and ears. Brooklyn Museum, New York.
Nayarit is a state on the west coast of Mexico, with Tapic as its capital. It is difficult to group clay figures from this region into periods, but they are all unquestionably pre-Columbian.

14 Head of a Yoruba wood-carving from Nigeria, Africa
    Carlebach Gallery, New York.
This tribe worked in a forceful style which developed from ancient West African cultural roots.

15 Head of a clay figure from Western Mexico (Nayarit)
    Worcester Art Museum, Worcester, Mass.
Clay figures from this region probably date from somewhere between 500 and 1500. See note on plate 13.

16 Head of a Baule wood-carving, Africa
    University Museum, Philadelphia.
This delicate, noble face is especially notable for the fine treatment of the hair-style and artistic reproduction of the tattooing. The Baule tribe belongs to the Aqui race on the Ivory Coast of West Africa.

17/18 Guardian figures of the Bakota, Africa
    Wooden centre with metal mountings. Carlebach Gallery, New York.
Some of these highly-civilised heads are convex, others are concave, and many have two faces. If asked about these contrasts, the Bakota tribesman would answer: 'One man's meat is another man's poison.'

19 Head of a Gothic Madonna, Spain
    Fourteenth century. Worcester Art Museum, Worcester, Mass.

20 Head of St Catherine of Siena, Italy
    Late fifteenth century. Metropolitan Museum of Art, New York.
A singularly impressive expression of Christian feeling, conforming with the Renaissance ideal of beauty.

21 Head of a Gothic Madonna, Northern Spain
    Limestone, fourteenth century. Metropolitan Museum of Art, New York.
Gothic art in Spain was at first subject to French influence; later, it acquired the stamp of Italy and the Netherlands.

II THE ETERNAL POSE

22 Clay figure from Ur, Babylon
    2000 B.C. The University Museum, Philadelphia.
Presumably a fertility goddess. During the third millennium B.C. Ur was the capital of Babylon and flourished through sea trade.

23 Archaic female figure from Cyprus
    2000 B.C. Museum of Fine Arts, Boston.
Cypriot culture shows traces of Aegean, Asian, Mesopotamian and Egyptian influence. The goddess Aphrodite came from this part of the world and was, therefore, also known as Cypris.

24 *Terra-cotta figure from Tel Yedeideh, Northern Syria*
About 2900 B.C. Museum of Fine Arts, Boston.
The Uruk culture in the Sumerian civilisation of Northern Syria was followed by the Jemdet Nasr period of the temple rulers.

25 *Goddess of fertility from Iran*
Fourth century B.C. Metropolitan Museum of Art, New York.
During the fourth century Artaxerxes III, who conquered Egypt in 342, ruled the Persian kingdom, which reached from the Mediterranean to the Indus. Under Darius III the kingdom succumbed to the onslaught of Alexander the Great.

26 *Terra-cotta figure of Demeter, Greece*
Fifth century B.C. Museum of Fine Arts, Boston.
The Eleusinian Mysteries, celebrated twice yearly by the Greeks, were based in part on the veneration of Demeter, the goddess of agriculture and fertility.

27 *Ancestral figure from the coastal belt of the Cameroons*
Wood-carving from the Bamende region, nineteenth century. American Museum of Natural History, New York.
Although the positioning of the hands is not uncommon among Negro carvings, it is less usual in the Cameroons than elsewhere.

28 *Ivory figure from the Luba tribe, Africa*
Ex-Belgian Congo. Brooklyn Museum, New York.
May influences of a highly-developed culture perhaps have filtered into the jungle? Female figures of this kind—always of the highest quality—are typical of this tribe, which itself once owned an extensive kingdom.

29 *Marble figure from the Cyclades*
Third millennium B.C. Metropolitan Museum of Art, New York.
See note on plate 1.

30 *The Medici Venus, Greece*
(Cast; original in the Uffizi, Florence.)
The Medici Venus was adapted from a Greek statue of Aphrodite during the time of the Roman Empire and was reproduced countless times during both Roman times and the Renaissance.

31 *Archaic figure from Cyprus*
Museum of Fine Arts, Boston.
The way the hands are disposed suggests a goddess of fertility. See note on plate 23.

32 *Lava figure from Las Mercedes, Costa Rica, Central America*
Brooklyn Museum, New York. About twelfth century.
It is remarkable that even the figures of the pre-Columbian civilisations in the New World show the familiar positioning of the hands. In all probability this, too, is a fertility figure.

33 *Wooden figure from Africa*
Nineteenth century. American Museum of Natural History, New York.
The origin of this figure is unknown. However, it is certainly over a hundred years old, which is a great age in view of Africa's destructive climate and insects. The attitude is identical with that of statues thousands of years older. Doubtless this is another fertility idol.

34 *Wooden Ba-Kongo figure, Africa*
Carlebach Gallery, New York.
The age-old convention of the hands offering the breast has survived in the art of primitive societies, as this contemporary statue shows.

35 *Ancestral figure in Taomiro wood from Easter Island*
American Museum of Natural History, New York.
Easter Island is the furthest eastward of the Polynesian Islands. The collapse of the old Polynesian civilisation came in 1750. Most characteristic are the huge statues of black tufa found there.

36 *Medici-type Venus, Greece*
Roman copy in bronze, first century B.C. Museum of Fine Arts, Boston.
See note on plate 30.

37 *The Egyptian Mother Goddess, Isis*
Glazed earthenware figure, about 12.5 cm. high. 26th—30th dynasty. (663—341 B.C.) Metropolitan Museum of Art, New York.
Motherhood was symbolised in Egyptian art by Isis and her marital and sisterly relationship with Osiris. The 26th dynasty saw a revival of the arts and crafts in Ancient Egypt.

III MOTHERHOOD

38 Ivory statue of Madonna and Child, France
   End of fourteenth century. Metropolitan Museum of Art, New York.
The figure's motherliness and human quality, which scarcely suggest any longer the remote Queen of Heaven, were emulated in many works.

39 Bronze statue of the young Krishna, India
   About 1800. Metropolitan Museum of Art, New York.
Here Krishna is shown being nursed by his mother, Dewaki. Krishna was worshipped throughout India, and his holy places were in Mathura, Dwaraka and Puri.

40 Mother goddess from Ur, Babylon
   Second millennium B. C. University Museum, Philadelphia.
Around 2000, the worship of the mother goddess in Ur gradually yielded to that of the god-king.

41 Goddess of fertility from the Bena Lulua, Africa
   Ex-Belgian Congo. Brooklyn Museum, New York.
This carving is probably the finest of its kind existing in America.

42 Terra-cotta figure from the Mexican highlands of Tlatilco
   About 1000 B. C. D'Arcy Galleries, New York.
Female figures, occasionally with a child, were frequently found in the highlands. They are in all probability fertility goddesses, for one rarely encounters them in tombs, more often in the fields.

43 Terra-cotta figure in Colima style, Mexico
   Pre-Columbian. Peabody Museum, Cambridge, Mass.
The province of Colima lies on the Pacific coast of Mexico, with the present town of Manzamillo as its capital.

44 Terra-cotta figure, Toltec, Mexico
   Pre-Columbian. Museum of Primitive Art, New York.
Mexican clay figurines, like African sculptures, show distinctive local and tribal styles.

45 Bronze statues from the Gio tribe, Liberia
   Peabody Museum, Cambridge, Mass.

46 Carving from Melanesia
   Nineteenth century. Museum of Primitive Art, New York.
This peculiar figure was carved by the natives living around Lake Santani before 1875 (a great age for any wooden object from tropical regions). It is a particularly rare piece, full of secrets even for the ethnologist, for throughout Melanesia nothing similar has ever been found. Its significance within the cult is not known.

47 Wood-carving from the Ba-Kongo, Africa
   Lower Congo. Brooklyn Museum, New York.
The theme of mother and child was popular among the Ba-Kongo tribe. The hollow in the child's body is significant; in it was placed the magical object which gave the figure the nature of a fetish. The figure could only serve this purpose with the assistance of a medicine man.

48 Baule wood-carving, Africa
   Ivory Coast. University Museum, Philadelphia.
One of this tribe's most delightful works. The mother carries the older child on her back while the younger greedily sucks at the breast.

49 *Wooden figure from the Senufo, Africa*
Western Sudan to Ivory Coast. D'Arcy Galleries, New York.

Over-emphasis of the breasts, the source of nourishment, is a particular feature of West African carvings.

50 *Indian mother and child*
Museum of Primitive Art, New York.

This Indian mother seems to fix us with a grave, unyielding gaze, while lovingly offering her child the breast, which the child tenderly presses. It is a unique composition for the cultures of the north-west coast of North America.

51 *Isis, the Egyptian goddess of fertility, with her son, Horus*
Third century B.C. Ptolemaic period. Metropolitan Museum of Art, New York.

The face of the goddess expresses maternal pride; her humanity lives on in many statues of the Madonna.

52 *Ashanti wood-carving, Africa*
Gold Coast. D'Arcy Galleries, New York.

53 *English Madonna*
Fourteenth century. D'Arcy Galleries, New York.

She reigns in supreme and unbending majesty; her robe is conventional. These traits, however, are softened by the way in which she holds the Christ Child and offers Him her breast.

54 *Swedish Madonna of the late Middle Ages*
Enanger's Kyrokomuseum, Haelsingland, Sweden.

This Madonna by the wood-carver Haakon Gulleson gives the impression of being a trifle stiff and severe, a peasant queen.

55 *Marble statue of Madonna and Child, France*
Mid-fourteenth century. Metropolitan Museum of Art, New York.

The Franco-Flemish style is characterized by charming elegance. The hand of the Madonna and the folds of the cloth should be noted. Lovingly the Christ Child touches the left cheek of His mother; the artist has stressed the human element above the divine.

56 *Burgundian sculpture*
About 1500. Metropolitan Museum of Art, New York.

The strongest impression given by this sculpture is of a happy human mother, rather than the embodiment of a religious idea.

57 *Stone statue by Robert Moir*
Whitney Museum of American Art, New York.

IV PROVOCATION AND VANITY

58 *Wooden statue of Mary Magdalene, Germany*
About 1520. Metropolitan Museum of Art, New York.

This era favoured the portrayal of saints in the elegantly-fashioned robes of the period.

59 *Stone sculpture from Egypt*
18th dynasty, around 1400 B.C. Museum of Fine Arts, Boston.

Fashionable accessories, the sumptuous wig and the jewellery around the neck, reveal the noble station of this Egyptian woman of the New Kingdom.

60 *Baule wood-carving, Africa*
Ivory Coast. University Museum, Philadelphia.
Inevitably, this carving demands comparison with the Egyptian statue on the opposite page. Here too, the hair-style shows artificial elaboration. The rich tattooing on the head and body has a like fashionable significance.

61 *Head of a wooden statue from the Krã (Liberia), Africa*
Peabody Museum, Cambridge, Mass.
The neck ornaments show that for the women of this tribe rows of heavy copper rings were a sign of fashionable wealth, although this type of jewellery was probably most uncomfortable to wear.

62 *Back view of a wooden statue from the Baule, Africa*
Ivory Coast. D'Arcy Galleries, New York.
This carving shows how patiently and meticulously the fastidious African woman dresses her hair.

63 *Babembe wood-carving, Africa*
Carlebach Gallery, New York.
The figures of the Babembe tribe from the Lower Congo have a forceful, fascinating originality. The large head and careful reproduction of the tattooing characterize them as typical African sculpture. The figure gives the impression that it is waiting to spring from the uncanny undergrowth of the jungle.

64 *Head of a Baule wood-carving, Africa*
D'Arcy Galleries, New York.
A quite unusual hair-style which must have demanded much time and effort.

65 *Wooden figure from the Bakuba, Africa*
Central Congo region. American Museum of Natural History, New York.
The Bakuba are one of the most interesting and artistic tribes in the Congo. Both male and female figures show the same stern facial expressions, which lends them a remoteness and dignity, at its best in the famous statues of the tribal kings.

66 *Tchambuli wood-carving, New Guinea*
American Museum of Natural History, New York.
These figures, painted with ritual patterns, are from Melanesia. Here, female figures are far more rare than male. For certain festivals in honour of the Earth Mother or the legendary ancestress, some female figures were carved, but they were always kept by the men of the village.

67 *Tattooed wooden figure from the Baluba, Africa*
University Museum, Philadelphia.
Many African tribes practise the custom of tattooing; the designs sometimes correspond remarkably to ornaments which they also use in their art. This particularly applies to the Baluba tribe in the Congo.

68 *Base of a chieftain's throne from the Bena Kanioka, Africa*
Ex-Belgian Congo. Peabody Museum, Cambridge, Mass.
Note the elaborate cicatrization of the abdomen of the crouching figure.

69 *Wooden mask from the Makonde in Tanganyika, Africa*
Carlebach Gallery, New York.
This mask is typical of the Makonde tribe, one of the few in East Africa whose art compares favourably with that of West Africa or the Congo.

70 *Head of a wood-carving from the Baule, Africa*
Ivory Coast. Carlebach Gallery, New York.
Yet another example of the importance attached by this tribe to the styling of the hair. (See notes on plates 62 and 64.)

71 *Senufo wood-carving, Africa*
Museum of Primitive Art, New York.
This towering hair-style can still be found among the women of the Senufo tribe on the Ivory Coast.

72 *Terra-cotta figure from India*
1000—300 B.C. Museum of Fine Arts, Boston.
Despite its diminutive proportions ($4^3/8$ in. in height), this figure has been carved with great respect for detail and is profusely ornamented. It comes from the province of Mathura, a centre for Indian art.

73 *Bronze statue of the Indian goddess Parwati*
Twelfth to thirteenth century. Worcester Art Museum, Worcester, Mass.
Parwati (Daughter of the Mountains) is the wife of Shiva. She is also called Durga (The Unapproachable), which indicates that she is the daughter of the Himalayas.

74 *Head of a terra-cotta figure from the West Coast of Mexico*
Pre-Columbian. Peabody Museum, Cambridge, Mass.
Such vigorous figures with their lively faces are typical of the province of Nayarit. The adornment of nose-ring and the sumptuous ear ornaments are vividly reproduced.

V ABSTRACT FORMS AND DISTORTIONS

75 The 'Venus of Willendorf', Aurignacian
30,000 B.C. Krems, Lower Austria. (Cast).

This limestone statuette is the most famous, and also one of the earliest, religious figures of the Stone Age hunters from Central Europe. It is not quite 4³/₈ in. in height. A remarkable feature is the representation of the hair. Of all the female figures shown in this book, those from the Stone Age are the strangest and most mysterious, for excavations never brought to light any clues to a particular cult. It is almost certain that the figures are of fertility goddesses. The name 'Venuses' or 'Venus statuettes', given to these Early Stone Age creations, is misleading but in common use.

76 Early Stone Age idol, Aurignacian
(Cast).

This figure, which is scarcely 1¹/₈ in. high, was found in the cave of Baoussé-Roussé near Menton.

77 'Venus I of Dolní Věstonice', Czechoslovakia
20,000 B.C. (Cast).

The bust and buttocks of this figure, approximately 3¹/₂ in. high, are rather less exaggerated. It, too, shows the unmistakable Aurignacian style.

78 Fertility idol from Menton, Aurignacian
(Cast).

As this 3 in.-high statuette shows, many features of the Upper Palaeolithic style are seen to best advantage in profile, in particular the thin, body-hugging arms. The figure portrayed is that of a pregnant woman.

79 Mexican statuette of a pregnant woman
Pre-Columbian. American Museum of Natural History, New York.

A clay figure from Nayarit, separated from the figure on the previous page by continents and thousands of years. Its realism is remarkable: it gives the impression that the woman feels the hour of birth drawing near and therefore squats in readiness.

80/81 Terra-cotta 'dancers' of the Egyptian pre-dynastic period
About 3,000 B.C. Brooklyn Museum, New York.

These figures with their bird-like faces are evidently precursors of the later traditional Egyptian art. The significance of these burial gifts is unknown. One is tempted to think of a religious dance performed by anthropomorphic deities, who visit and accompany the dead.

82 Marble idol from the Cyclades
2000 B.C. D'Arcy Galleries, New York.

In its art, hardly any ancient epoch tended so strongly towards the abstract as did the Cycladic culture of the Aegean.

83 Marble idol from the Cyclades
3000 B.C. Worcester Art Museum, Worcester, Mass.

This example of the mysterious culture of the Cyclades, which we of the present day find particularly fascinating, possesses a face that is almost the last word in abstract treatment, while that of the body and, in particular, the folded arms is delicately realistic.

84 Clay figurine from Syria
2000 B.C. Metropolitan Museum of Art, New York.

This and the other figurines from archaic civilizations that follow were for the most part conceived as votive offerings, and were buried in the ground. Such rigidly-stylized, bird-like faces and outstretched arms are characteristic of the Near East.

85 Clay figures of the pre-Maurja culture in Northern India
Second millennium B.C. Museum of Fine Arts, Boston.

Ancient artistic traditions were not readily lost, as is shown by this figurine, which is similar to earlier ones in gesture, facial expression and opulent ornamentation.

86 Bronze Age figure from Iran
About 2000 B.C. University Museum, Philadelphia.

This well-preserved figure, almost 9⁷/₈ in. high, was found in a tomb in Turang-Tepe. The emphasis on the swelling breasts, the narrow waist and the broad hips suggests Indian influence.

87 *Fertility idol from Iraq*
2000 B.C. Metropolitan Museum of Art, New York.
The hips and thighs of this figure are emphasized by impressed strokes, perhaps representing a type of apron. These figures usually have sumptuous hair-styles and jewellery.

88 *Pre-dynastic terra-cotta idol from Egypt*
Third millennium B.C. Metropolitan Museum of Art, New York.
The combination of human and animal features, so common in later Egyptian deities, is already noticeable in this small pre-dynastic clay figure. Here, too, a representation of fertility is undoubtedly intended; with an unmistakable gesture the goddess offers her breasts as a symbol of fruitfulness.

89 *Egyptian terra-cotta idols*
Pre-dynastic. University Museum, Philadelphia.
The erect stance and zoomorphic faces point to Egyptian art, but other characteristics suggest that these figures were imported. Between even the earliest civilizations trade was widespread.

90 *Alabaster figure from Iran*
1500 B.C. University Museum, Philadelphia.
This small figure shows what enormous variety there was in the early Iranian cultures. Only the raised arms are reminiscent of other pieces; its strongly-stylized face has no points of comparison with them.

91 *Clay idols from Mycenae*
1400 B.C. Brooklyn Museum, New York.
A relationship to pre-dynastic Egyptian clay figures is indicated above all by the severe poses, although thousands of years separate these figures, found in a Mycenaean grave, from anything Egyptian. The angular, bird-like faces and the roughly-suggested outlines of the body are characteristic.

92 *Prehistoric idol of the Harappa culture, India*
2000 B.C. Museum of Fine Arts, Boston.
The ruins of the first great cities of India—Harappa and Mohenjo-Daro on the Indus—are most imposing. Their alphabet has not yet been deciphered, but their culture seems to have been influenced by Sumer. Beside polished sculpture, reminiscent of Greek art, they have yielded roughly-made clay figures like this one, whose faces with their round eyes and beak-like profile remind one of birds. It is uncertain whether these are divine idols or toys.

93 *Bronze Age terra-cotta figurine from Mathura, India*
1000—300 B.C. Museum of Fine Arts, Boston.
This figurine suggests a fertility goddess. Mathura is one of the oldest centres of Indian art. Sculptures in red sandstone, especially, can be traced from the third century B.C. up to the sixth century A.D.

94 *Terra-cotta figure from Chupicuaro, Mexico*
Early Huaxtec style, pre-Columbian. Peabody Museum, Cambridge, Mass.
The Huaxtecs belong to the Maya group. Almost all pre-Columbian Mexican clay sculpture is typified by abundant decoration, while the pierced ears for inserting wooden pins were favoured in both Central and South America.

95 *Prehistoric terra-cotta figurine from Missouri, U.S.A.*
American Museum of Natural History, New York.
The sculptures from the central and southern United States are simpler and more cubic than those from Mexico. The burial mounds in Missouri yielded numerous finds of a mysterious Indian civilization which had perished long before the arrival of Columbus. This figure suggests a definite religious purpose.

96 *Terra-cotta idol from Tepic, Mexico*
Pre-Columbian. Peabody Museum, Cambridge, Mass.
This small figure, which may represent a pregnant woman kneeling, was found in a tomb in the region of Tepic, the capital of the state of Nayarit, in Western Mexico. The face is hardly formed, the body highly stylized.

97 *Terra-cotta idol from Vera Cruz, Mexico*
Huaxtec style, pre-Columbian. American Museum of Natural History, New York.
The sculptures from the civilizations along the coast of the Mexican Gulf have all the luxuriance of the tropics, and are characterized by squat, sturdy, bulging bodies and elaborate head-dresses.

98 *Terra-cotta figure in the style of Colima, Western Mexico*
300 to 1000. University Museum, Philadelphia.
The province of Colima is situated on the Pacific coast of Mexico. Like Jalisco and several other provinces, it produced a style of its own. This female figurine with long, centre-parted hair is covered from waist to knees with elaborate body decoration.

99 *Terra-cotta figure from the region of Vera Cruz, Mexico*
Pre-Columbian. University Museum, Philadelphia.
The clumsiness of this figure, without any characteristic decorations or head deformity, makes it difficult to assign it to a culture or era. One may assume that it had ritual significance as a goddess of fertility.

100 *North-American Indian clay figure, Missouri, U.S.A.*
About 1450 to 1600. University Museum, Philadelphia.
This ritual urn in the shape of a woman originates from a burial mound in Missouri. It is an unusual work of art, portraying a female deity or ancestor figure.

101 *Tattooed wood-carving from the Kasai region, Africa*
Congo. American Museum of Natural History, New York.
This figure is an example of 'simple' carving. Not all African tribes were as artistic as, say, the Luba, but most of them needed such figures for their religious ceremonies and rites.

102 *Wooden Bambara idol, Africa*
Western Sudan. Museum of Primitive Art, New York.
The Bambara of the Western Sudan produce fascinating wooden figures. This example shows a stylized treatment, the effect of which is astonishingly powerful.

103 *Fetishes of the Wakwere, Africa*
Tanganyika. American Museum of Natural History, New York.
Sculptures in the round are very rare in East Africa. Several of the Bantu tribes live, even today, almost completely cut off from the many influences to which the coastal regions have been exposed. They produce simple carvings, such as these highly-stylized figures of the Wakwere. They were conceived as magical figures, hence their un-naturalistic form.

104 *Bambara goddess of fertility, Africa*
Western Sudan. Brooklyn Museum, New York.
Although betraying a definite and common style, the sculptures of any one tribe still vary considerably, as this detail from a Bambara figure shows when compared with others from the same source.

105 *Fetish of the Fang Tribes, Africa*
Congo. Peabody Museum, Cambridge, Mass.
This figure has an aura of the shadow-world of sorcery and witchcraft.

106 *Terra-cotta figures in the Jalisco style of Mexico*
Pre-Columbian, 500—1500. Museum of Primitive Art, New York.
Such portrayals of women are typical of little-explored regions in the Mexican highlands, inhabited at the time of the Conquistadors by the independent and warlike Tarask tribe. The age of these figures is uncertain; they are vastly different from the works of the advanced civilizations in other parts of the highlands, and their significance is puzzling. Clay figures with stern, elongated faces are typical of the province of Jalisco. In West Mexico the reproduction of the naked female form—with the exception of a few goddesses—is very rare. The peculiar button-like discs on the shoulders are found on many Jalisco figures. These statuettes may symbolize illnesses.

107 *Clay figures of the Huaxtecs, Mexico*
Before 200. Peabody Museum, Cambridge, Mass.
The figure on the right with its slanting eyes and exaggerated brow may originate from the west of the Mexican Gulf; that on the left is very strange and its origin is difficult to determine. Common to both figures are holes for the typical wooden ear pins.

108 *Bronze Age idols, Sweden*
1200 B.C.
In contrast to the Egyptian 'dancers' (plates 80, 81) these figures from the Bronze Age in Sweden suggest ancient goddesses; the bodies are awkwardly fashioned, all unnecessary detail being dispensed with. The head of the figure on the left in particular bears a distinct resemblance to that of the figure on plate 1.

109 *Ashanti goddesses of fertility, Africa*
Gold Coast. D'Arcy Galleries, New York.
The Ashanti of West Africa are famous for their highly-naturalistic brass castings. Therefore, these figures with their disc-like faces seem particularly strange. Imbued with a deep significance, they are carried by young women anxious for the gift of a child.

110 *Painted figures from the Caraja Indians, Brazil*
American Museum of Natural History, New York.
These unfired clay figures from the Caraja Indians of Brazil were probably used as toys. They are dressed up with rags and pieces of bark—probably the reason why most of them are armless.

111   Tanagra figures, Greece
   Boeotia. Fourth century B.C. Museum of Fine Arts,
   Boston.

All antiquity was familiar with clay figures as votive offerings, as burial gifts and as children's toys. For the most part they were simple, coarse products, but some of them show fine workmanship. The figures found since about 1870 in the tombs near the Greek city of Tanagra in Boeotia are famous. Copies of originals in Athens, they provide us with a vivid picture of the Greeks from the end of the fourth century until Hellenistic times.

112   Terra-cotta figure from La Mata Maracay, Venezuela
   American Museum of Natural History, New York.

These fantastic clay figures, only 4–5¹/₂ in. high, are from Venezuela. As yet, nothing is known about their age, particularly since figures in this style are found in regions as far apart as the north coast of Venezuela and the southern half of Central America.

VI   THE TORSO

113   Torso of Aphrodite, Greece
   Metropolitan Museum of Art, New York.

Hellenistic copy, first century B.C., of a fourth-century Greek original.

114   Guitou Knoop: Torso

This sculptress was born in Moscow in 1902. She was in Paris as a pupil of Bourdelle in 1927; since 1948 she has favoured rather more abstract creations. Guitou Knoop divides her time between Paris and New York.

115   Terra-cotta torso from Atzcapotzalco, Mexico
   Huaxtec civilization of Central America. Pre-Columbian. Peabody Museum, Cambridge, Mass.

The fluidity of the body formation and exotic charm compensate for the fact that the statue is no longer complete.

116   Egyptian limestone torso
   4th dynasty (2680—2560 B.C.) Worcester Art Museum,
   Worcester, Mass.

This life-size figure was sculptured during one of the great periods of Egyptian art. During the 4th dynasty (Old Kingdom) the pyramid builders, Sneferu, Cheops, Chephren, and Mycerinus, were at work. This statue, too, is the work of a great master.

117   Hellenistic torso of Hygeia, Greece
   Second century B.C. Worcester Art Museum, Worcester, Mass.

The statue of Hygeia, goddess of health, with her elaborately-carved garment, was found in Antioch on the Orontes. It may be a later copy of the second-century original.

*118   Torso of a Torana figure from the Great Stupa in Sanchi,
   Central India*
   First century B.C. Museum of Fine Arts, Boston.

This figure is one of the earliest large sculptures preserved in India. 'Stupa' is the name given, particularly in Ceylon, to a sacred building housing relics.

119   Gaston Lachaise: Torso
   Museum of Modern Art, New York.

The 'intentional' torso is a product of modern art. The head is deliberately ignored in order to heighten the effect of the body. Gaston Lachaise was born in Paris in 1882 and emigrated to America in 1906. He died in New York in 1935.

120   Alberto Viani: Torso
   Museum of Modern Art, New York.

Viani's style, although tending towards the abstract, still shows plainly the essential parts of the female body. Alberto Viani, born in Questello (Mantua) in 1906, teaches at the Academy of Art in Venice.

VII CLASSIC FORMS

121 Bronze nymph by Germain Pilon (1535—1590)
Museum of Fine Arts, Boston.

The fountain of which the nymph shown here forms part is ascribed to Germain Pilon. Pilon's creations, like those of Goujon, conform to the ideal of his age, which was consciously inspired by the art of antiquity.

122 Silver statuette of an Egyptian noblewoman
Ptolemaic age (323—30 B.C.) Metropolitan Museum of Art, New York.

The unwavering look, worldly-wise and vivacious, no longer leaves room for any suggestion of sacred associations. Under the Ptolemies, Egypt became the richest country in the world.

123 Bronze figure of the Egyptian goddess Neith, the heavenly goddess of Sais
26th dynasty (663—525 B.C.). Metropolitan Museum of Art, New York.

Neith, or Neret, is the mother of the gods, the first woman to bear a child. She was worshipped in Sais and later in Esna, where the latos fish was sacred to her. The later work has a much more vivid, playful and natural effect than the severe, noble torso of the 4th dynasty (see plate 116).

124 Ivory carving from the palace of Kalhu (Nimrûd), Assyria
Metropolitan Museum of Art, New York.

Still blackened by the fire, these purely ornamental figures from the palace, burnt down in 715 B.C. by invaders, reflect something of the Assyrian ideal of beauty.

125 Stone figure of a fertility goddess from Ur, Babylon
About 2000 B.C. University Museum, Philadelphia.

During the third millennium, Ur was the capital of Babylon, and, through its sea trade, enjoyed a golden age.

126 Statue of Aphrodite
Metropolitan Museum of Art, New York.

See note on plate 113.

127 Etruscan bronze figure
Third century B.C. Museum of Fine Arts, Boston.

This figure is in some measure related to the Greek statue of the preceding plate; but the impression it gives is one of greater strength and, despite its slimness and elegant pose, of provinciality.

128 Bronze statuette of Parwati, India
Fifteenth century. Museum of Fine Arts, Boston.

Parwati, the wife of the Hindu god, Shiva, is usually portrayed in clearly-defined dance attitudes; here, her right hand is raised in the gesture of Kataku-Mudra, her left is lowered in that of Lola-Mudra.

129 Bambara statuette, Africa
Sudan. Museum of Primitive Art, New York.

Here, a translation into the geometric abstract has been effected with unerring feeling for anatomy.

130 Wooden statuette of Lucretia, Germany
Beginning of the sixteenth century. Metropolitan Museum of Art, New York.

The portrayal of Lucretia committing suicide was a popular theme of the German Renaissance. It provided an opportunity to combine the beauty of the female body with the drama of death. This statuette of box-wood, about $8^5/_8$ in. high, was probably the work of a lesser South German master.

131 'Diane de Poitiers' by Jean Goujon (c. 1515—1564/8), France
Much has been written about Goujon's sculptures. One of his most distinguished models was Henry II's mistress, who posed for this 'classically' orientated statue.

132 Life-size bronze figure by Doris Caesar
Much of the powerful effect of this semi-abstract work by the contemporary American sculptress is due to the elongation of head, neck and limbs.

VIII WOMAN IN MODERN SCULPTURE

133 Wilhelm Lehmbruck (1881—1919): Kneeling woman
Museum of Modern Art, New York.
Lehmbruck's mature works often show strangely elongated proportions; these are indicative of the artist's lifelong striving for a new spatial function of the figure, and bestowed upon his sculptures, a genuine spirituality bordering on the sacred.

134 Edgar Degas (1834—1917): Dancer
Baltimore Art Museum.
Degas's few sculptures possess superlative charm. One is tempted to call them 'Hellenistic', for a frequent characteristic is the attempt to capture movement.

135 Aristide Maillol (1861—1944): L'action enchainée
Metropolitan Museum of Art, New York.
In the field of representational art Maillol emerges as the most classical sculptor of modern times. He adds French charm to concise Greek severity. His works had a world-wide influence.

136 Henri Laurens (1885—1954): Woman seated
Private collection, New York.
Primarily, Laurens was influenced by Rodin. In 1911 he encountered Braque and the Cubist movement, and executed coloured sculptures. He was never an abstract sculptor; after 1930 his female figures in particular became monumental and compact. He later took up mythological themes.

137 Marino Marini (born 1901): Pomona III, 1943
Private collection, New York.
Marini has created both groups and numerous portraits. He is particularly well-known for his 'Horse and Rider' series.

138 Henri Matisse (1869—1954): Woman reclining, 1907
Private collection, New York.
The great painter and leading representative of the 'Fauves' created many sculptures, which became more and more confined to essentials; they throw a new light on the rest of the master's works.

139 Antoine Pevsner (born 1886): Half figure of a woman
Private collection, New York.
Born in Orel, Russia, Pevsner was at an early stage influenced by Byzantine architecture and icons. With his brother, Naum Gabo, he joined in the *avant-garde* movement in art. In company with Kandinsky and Malevitsch, he taught at the Academy of Art in Moscow. Since 1923 he has lived in Paris, where his first large exhibition was held in 1947.

140 Henry Moore (born 1898): Woman reclining
Private collection, New York.
Moore has created numerous monumental works for public places. He combines the abstract with the representational; his disrupted figures never belie the forms of the human body.

141 Henry Moore: Woman reclining.
Museum of Modern Art, New York.

142 Pablo Picasso (born 1881): Bronze figure
Picasso's early sculptures were produced at the beginning of this century. The influence of Negro art led to Cubist forms. After several Constructivist creations he returned to representational works.

143 Pablo Picasso: Three female figures
Without inspiration from primitive art it is unlikely that either these figures or the preceding bronze would have been created. Nevertheless they are an expression of our age and our civilisation.

ACKNOWLEDGMENTS

Most of the sculptures in this book were photographed in the following museums, to which grateful acknowledgment is made: The American Museum of Natural History, New York; The Brooklyn Museum, Brooklyn; The Metropolitan Museum of Art, New York; The Museum of Modern Art, New York; The Museum of Primitive Art, New York; The Whitney Museum of American Art, New York; Museum of Fine Arts, Boston, Mass; Peabody Museum of Anthropology and Ethnology, Cambridge, Mass; The University Museum, Philadelphia, Pa; Worcester Art Museum, Worcester, Mass.